Table of Contents

INTRODUCTION

The word "fermentation" has undergone many changes in meaning during the past hundred years. According to the derivation of the term, it signifies merely a gentle bubbling or boiling condition. The term was first applied when the only known reaction of this kind was the production of wine, the bubbling, of course, being caused by the production of carbon dioxide.

It was not until Gay-Lussac studied the chemical aspects of the process that the meaning was changed to signify the breakdown of sugar into ethanol and carbon dioxide (316). It was Pasteur, however, who marked the birth of chemical microbiology with his association of microbes with fermentation in 1857. He used the terms "cell" and "ferment" interchangeably in referring to the microbe. The term "fermentation" thus became associated with the idea of cells, gas production, and the production of organic byproducts.

The evolution of gas and the presence of whole cells were invalidated as criteria for defining fermentation when it was discovered that in some fermentations, such as the production of lactic acid, no gas is liberated. Moreover, other fermentation processes could be obtained with cell-free extracts indicating that the whole cell may not be necessary.

The position was further complicated by the discovery that the ancient process of vinegar production, generally referred to as acetic acid fermentation, which yielded considerable quantities of organic byproducts, was a strictly aerobic process. Fermentation clearly needed to be redefined.

Although carbohydrates are often regarded as essential materials for fermentations, organic acids (including amino acids) and proteins, fats, and other organic compounds are fermentable substrates for selected microorganisms. It was soon realized that these substances play a dual role as a source of food and as a source of energy for the microorganisms (375). The energy produced by total combustion (oxidation) of the substance in a calorimeter is its potential energy. The nearest approach to complete oxidation biologically occurs with acidic oxidations, which, with glucose, yield carbon dioxide and water and result in the liberation of a considerable quantity of energy.

Under anaerobic conditions, only a fraction of the potential energy is liberated because oxidation is incomplete. In order to obtain an amount of energy equivalent to that obtained under aerobic conditions, several times as much glucose must be broken down under anaerobic conditions. There is, in consequence, a high yield of unoxidized organic byproduct.

Fermentation came to be regarded, then, as the anaerobic decomposition of organic compounds to organic products, which could not be further metabolized by the enzyme systems of the cells without the intervention of oxygen. The fermentation products differed with different microorganisms, being governed in the main by the enzyme complex of the cells and the environmental conditions. The economic value of these byproducts led to the development of industrial microbiology.

With the recognition of fermentation as an anaerobic process, parallels were drawn between the biochemistry of microorganisms and that of mammalian tissues. Because the intermediates of the metabolism of glucose were found to be the same, it was postulated that all fermentation processes must follow similar paths. Consequently, the microbial fermentation of carbohydrates was considered to be similar to mammalian glycolysis. This is why many authors use the terms "glycolysis" or "glycolytic pathway" to describe one method of anaerobic breakdown of carbohydrates by microorganisms and why "fermentation" became synonymous with "glycolysis." The two processes differ, however, in two significant ways: (1) there is no storage of glycogen in bacteria, and (2) lactate is not always an end product or intermediate in the bacterial anaerobic breakdown of carbohydrates. In addition, during the 1950's it was discovered that various bacteria are able to use pathways other than the Embden-Meyerhof-Parnas pathway for anaerobic breakdown of carbohydrates. The application of "fermentation" to all of these processes required some other form of definition.

The intensive research into electron transport systems of microbial metabolism has partly clarified the position, although a number of aspects await attention. From research on the electron donor and acceptor systems, it is now clearly understood that all processes which have as a terminal electron acceptor an organic compound are called "fermentations." With this definition, it is possible to state that acetic acid bacteria are not fermentative but respire aerobically. For other bacteria the definition is not restricted to the use of any particular pathway in the fermentative process.

It was also found that fermentative bacteria may dispense with the use of their cytochromes under anaerobic conditions, for their phosphorylation processes are substrate phosphorylations in which the electron donor is an organic substrate that transfers its electrons to an NAD+ or NADP+ system. The amount of NAD+ in microorganisms, however, is limited and NAD+ must therefore be regenerated if metabolism is to continue. Under anaerobic conditions, this regeneration can be accomplished by an oxidation–reduction mechanism involving pyruvate or other compounds derived from pyruvate. These reactions from pyruvate can vary considerably among microorganisms and therefore lead to the formation of characteristic end products that are used in bacterial classification.

Biologists use the term fermentation to describe anaerobic metabolism, the production of energy from nutrients without oxygen. Fermenting bacteria are thought to have emerged relatively early from the primordial prebiotic soup, before the atmosphere had a sufficient concentration of oxygen to support or evolve aerobic life-forms. "In the first two billion years of life on Earth, bacteria—the only inhabitants—continuously transformed the planet's surface and atmosphere and invented all of life's essential, miniaturized chemical systems," writes biologist Lynn Margulis.The research of Margulis and others has convinced many biologists that symbiotic relationships between fermenting bacteria and other early single-cell life-forms became permanently embodied as the first eukaryotic cells that plants, animals, and fungi comprise. As Margulis and Dorion

Sagan explain in their book Microcosmos, the symbiosis may have begun as a predator-prey relationship: Eventually some of the prey evolved a tolerance for their aerobic predators, whichthen remained alive and well in the food-rich interior of the host. Two types of organisms used the products of each other's metabolisms. As they reproduced inside the invaded cells without causing harm, the predators gave up their independent ways and moved in for good.

Evolution derived from such symbiosis is known as symbiogenesis. Microbiologists Sorin Sonea and Léo G. Mathieu elaborate on the concept: "Symbiogenesis with thousands of different bacterial genes has decisively enriched the limited metabolic potential of eukaryotic organisms, accelerating and facilitating their adaptation much more than would have been achieved by random mutation alone."

Bacterial fermentation processes have been part of the context for all life. Fermentation plays such a broad and vital role in nutrient cycling that all beings coevolved with it, ourselves included. Through symbiosis and coevolution, bacteria fused into new forms, spawning all other life. "For the past [billion] years, members of the Bacteria superkingdom have functioned as a major selective force shaping eukaryotic evolution," state molecular biologists Jian Xu and Jeffrey I. Gordon. "Coevolved symbiotic relationships between bacteria and multicellular organisms are a prominent feature of life on Earth." The importance of bacteria and our bacterial interactions cannot be overstated. We could not exist or function without our bacterial partners.

Even our reproduction requires fermentation. The human vagina has been found to secrete glycogen that supports an indigenous population of lactobacilli, which ferment the glycogen into lactic acid, thereby protecting the vagina from pathogenic bacteria, which cannot survive in an acid environment. "The presence of lactobacilli as a part of the normal vaginal flora is an important component of reproductive health." Our indigenous bacteria protect us everywhere and enable us to function in myriad ways that are just beginning to be understood. From an evolutionary perspective, this extensive microbiota "endows us with functional features that we have not had to evolve ourselves." This is a miracle of coevolution the bacteria that coexist with us in our bodies enable us to exist.

Microbiologist Michael Wilson notes that "each exposed surface of a human being is colonized by microbes exquisitely adapted to that particular environment." Yet the dynamics of these microbial populations, and how they interact with our bodies, are still largely unknown. A 2008 comparative genomics analysis of lactic acid bacteria acknowledges that research is "just now beginning to scratch the surface of the complex relationship between humans and their microbiota."

Bacteria are such effective coevolutionary partners because they are highly adaptable and mutable. "Bacteria continually monitor their external and internal environments and compute functional outputs based on information provided by their sensory apparatus,"explains bacterial geneticist James Shapiro, who reports "multiple widespread bacterial systems for mobilizing and engineering DNA molecules." In contrast with our eukaryotic cells, with fixed genetic material, prokaryotic bacteria have free-floating genes, which they frequently exchange. For this reason, some microbiologists consider it inappropriate to view bacteria as distinct species. "There are no species in prokaryotes," state Sorin Sonea and Léo G. Mathieu. "Bacteria are much more of a continuum," explains Lynn Margulis. "They just pick up genes, they throw away genes, and they are very flexible about that." Mathieu and Sonea describe a bacterial "genetic free market," in which "each bacterium can be compared to a two-way broadcasting station, using genes as information molecules." Genes "are carried by a bacterium only when needed as a human may carry sophisticated tools."

The emerging details of gene transfer are fascinating. In addition to exchanging genes directly with other bacteria, bacteria have receptors to receive genes from prophages, which Sonea and Mathieu call "a unique type of biological but inanimate construction: a micro-robot for gene exchanges organized like an ultramicroscopic syringe with a hollow container ('head'), and an ultramicroscopic needle ('tail'). This exclusively bacterial type of instrument for gene exchange among living beings may be carried across large distances by water, wind, animals, etc." With so many mechanisms for genetic exchange, "all the world's bacteria essentially have access to a single gene pool and hence to the adaptive mechanisms of the entire bacteria kingdom," summarize Margulis and Sagan. Beyond genetic flexibility, "bacteria utilise sophisticated mechanisms for intercellular communication and even have the ability to commandeer the basic cell biology of 'higher' plants and animals to meet their own needs," writes geneticist James Shapiro. A new understanding of bacteria is emerging; far from being simplistic "lower forms" of life, they are becoming recognized as highly evolved, with elaborate systems for adaptability and resilience.

Fermentation and Culture

What exactly is culture? In contrast with the realm of biological reproduction, where information is coded and copied as genes, in the cultural realm information is encoded as memes. Memes are transmitted through words, concepts, images, processes, abstractions—stories, pictures, books, films, photographs, computer programs, ledgers. Secret family recipes. Life lessons, like learning to identify edible plants, learning to garden, learning to cook, learning to fish, learning to procure, use, and preserve precious food resources. Fermenting.

It is largely our history of interacting with plants (and associated microbes) that gives rise to what we call "culture." After all, the word culture comes from Latin cultura, a form of the verb colere, to cultivate or till. The first definition of culture in the Oxford English Dictionary is simply: "The cultivation of land, and derived senses."

Through these derived senses, and the many varied manifestations of cultivation, ideas of what could be cultivated grew. People culture pearls, we culture cells, and we culture milk. We practice aquaculture, viticulture, and horticulture, not to mention popular culture. Many people work hard to imbue their children with culture. Sometimes people decry cultural appropriation or defend cultural purity. Culture begins with cultivating the land, planting seeds, bringing intentionality to cycles that we act to perpetuate. Indeed, a more ancient origin of the word culture is the Indo-European root kwel, meaning "to revolve," from which cycle, circle, chakra, and many other words, along with culture, are derived.35 Culture is

cultivation, but it is not an isolated act; it is, by definition, part of a cyclical ongoing process, passed from generation to generation.

As my exploration of fermentation unfolds, I keep coming back to the profound significance of the fact that we use the same word—culture—to describe the community of bacteria that transform milk into yogurt, as well as the practice of subsistence itself, language, music, art, literature, science, spiritual practices, belief systems, and all that human beings seek to perpetuate in our varied and overlapping collective existences. As described earlier, successful coexistence with microbes in our midst is a biological imperative, and the fermentation arts are human cultural manifestations of this essential fact. If we are to enjoy surpluses of food, then we must have strategies for preserving them in the presence of the microbial ecology, such as it is. Clearly, as a group, fermented foods and beverages are more than incidental culinary novelties; they appear to be found in some form in every culinary tradition. I have searched—without success—for examples of cultures that do not incorporate any form of fermentation. Indeed, ferments are central features of many, perhaps even most, cuisines. Immigrants crossing continents and oceans—their only belongings the ones they could carry—have often brought their sourdoughs and other starters with them, or at the very least their fermentation knowledge and practices. The fermentation starters themselves, and the knowledge of how to use them, are tangible embodiments of culture, deeply embedded in our desires and cravings, not lightly abandoned.

How can we even imagine the cultural realm without alcoholic beverages? Though some religions and nations ban alcohol altogether, thus defining themselves in opposition to it, alcohol is known and used everywhere, and of widespread importance in ritual, ceremony, and celebration. "Their preeminence and universal allure—what might be called their biological, social, and religious imperatives—make them significant in understanding the

development of our species and its cultures," states anthropologist Patrick E. McGovern, who has identified alcohol residues in 9,000- year-old pottery shards. "Our species' intimate relationship with fermented beverages over millions of years has, in large measure, made us what we are today."36 Most people seem to enjoy manipulating our gift and burden of consciousness, and do so by whatever means available. Alcohol has been far and away the most widely available and widely used intoxicant.

We do not know the origins of alcohol. The alcohol that Professor McGovern identified from the Neolithic settlement of Jiahu in China was made from a mixture of rice, honey, and fruit. It would appear that these early human alcohol makers were combining available carbohydrate and yeast sources, however they might have conceptualized the process. Is it possible that, rather than humans "discovering" alcohol and mastering its production, we evolved always already knowing it? Anthropologist Mikal John Aasved points out that "all vertebrate species are equipped with a hepatic enzyme system with which to metabolize alcohol." Many animals have been documented consuming alcohol in their natural habitats. One of them, a daily consumer of alcohol in the Malaysian jungle, is the pentailed treeshrew (Ptilocercus lowii). Interestingly, this mammal is considered to be "the morphologically least-derived living descendant of early ancestors of primates," regarded as a "living model" for the ancestral lineage from which primates radiated.

The alcohol these treeshrews consume occurs naturally on the bertram palm (Eugeissona tristis), on "specialized flower buds that harbor a fermenting yeast community." And the treeshrews are pollinators for the bertram palm. This tree, its pollinating shrews, and the fermenting yeast community all coevolved this arrangement together. It would be absurd to think of one species as the primary actor in this mutualistic community. As the primate family diverged from the treeshrews, it lost such highly specialized alcohol-laced relationships. But our primate and humanoid ancestors presumably ate lots of fruit, which ferments when ripe, especially quickly in the warm and wet jungle climate. Biologist Robert Dudley theorizes that our precursors were routinely exposed to alcohol in fruit, and that "this exposure in turn elicited corresponding physiological adaptations and preferences over an evolutionary time scale that are retained in modern humans." While alcohol is present in fruits at low concentrations compared with alcoholic beverages, the fleeting availability of seasonal fruits encourages gorging. I know I respond to plentiful ripe berries that way. And I am not unique in this regard. Addiction researcher

Ronald Siegel describes animals responding to fallen, split, fermenting durian fruits in Malaysia: A menagerie of jungle beasts, alerted by the ripening odor, parade to the fallen fruit. . . . Elephants that may have migrated from great distances sometimes gorge themselves on the fermented fruit remaining on the ground; they start swaying in a lethargic manner. The monkeys frequently lose motor coordination, have difficulty climbing, and start head-shaking. The flying foxes, which are the largest bats in the world and have the same tastes as humans, feed at night on mostly fermented and rotten fruit . . . [which] fouls the bat's sonar, thus causing navigational difficulties; the bats keep falling down and waddling on the ground.

Humans have taken advantage of the metabolism in a tiny fungus called yeast to create beer and wine from grains and fruits. What are the biological mechanisms behind this alcohol production?

Once upon a time, many, many years ago, a man found a closed fruit jar containing a honeybee. When he drank the contents, he tasted a new, strange flavor. Suddenly his head was spinning, he laughed for no reason, and he felt powerful. He drank all the liquid in the jar. The next day he experienced an awful feeling. He had a headache, pain, an unpleasant taste in his mouth, and dizziness — he had just discovered the hangover. You might think this is just a tale, but is it? Several archaeological excavations have discovered jars containing the remains of wine that are 7,000 years old, and it is very likely that humankind's first encounter with alcoholic beverages was by chance. How did this chance discovery lead to the development of the beer and wine industry and how did scientists eventually learn about the biological mechanisms of alcohol production?

The History of Beer and Wine Production

Over the course of human history, and using a system of trial, error, and careful observation, different cultures began producing fermented beverages. Mead, or honey wine, was produced in Asia during the Vedic period (around 1700–1100 BC), and the Greeks, Celts, Saxons, and Vikings also produced this beverage. In Egypt, Babylon, Rome, and China, people produced wine from grapes and beer from malted barley. In South America, people produced chicha from grains or fruits, mainly maize; while in North America, people made octli (now known as "pulque") from agave, a type of cactus.

At the time, people knew that leaving fruits and grains in covered containers for a long time produced wine and beer, but no one fully understood why the recipe worked. The process was named fermentation, from the Latin word fervere, which means "to boil." The name came from the observation that mixtures of crushed grapes kept in large vessels produced bubbles, as though they were boiling. Producing fermented beverages was tricky. If the mixture did not stand long enough, the product contained no alcohol; but if left for too long, the mixture rotted and was undrinkable. Through empirical observation, people learned that temperature and air exposure are key to the fermentation process.

Wine producers traditionally used their feet to soften and grind the grapes before leaving the mixture to stand in buckets. In so doing, they transferred microorganisms from their feet into the mixture. At the time, no one knew that the alcohol produced during fermentation was produced because of one of these microorganisms — a tiny, one-celled eukaryotic fungus that is invisible to the naked eye: yeast. It took several hundred years before quality lenses and microscopes revolutionized science and allowed researchers to observe these microorganisms.

Yeast and Fermentation

In the seventeenth century, a Dutch tradesman named Antoni van Leeuwenhoek developed high-quality lenses and was able to observe yeast for the first time. In his spare time Leeuwenhoek used his lenses to observe and record detailed drawings of everything he could, including very tiny objects, like protozoa, bacteria, and yeast. Leeuwenhoek discovered that yeast consist of globules floating in a fluid, but he thought they were merely the starchy particles of the grain from which the wort (liquid obtained from the brewing of whiskey and beer) was made (Huxley 1894). Later, in 1755, yeast were defined in the Dictionary of the English Language by Samuel Johnson as "the ferment put into drink to make it work; and into bread to lighten and swell it." At the time, nobody believed that yeast were alive; they were seen as just organic chemical agents required for fermentation.

In the eighteenth and nineteenth centuries, chemists worked hard to decipher the nature of alcoholic fermentation through analytical chemistry and chemical nomenclature. In 1789, the French chemist Antoine Lavoisier was working on basic theoretical questions about the transformations of substances. In his quest, he decided to use sugars for his experiments, and he gained new knowledge about their structures and chemical reactions. Using quantitative studies, he learned that sugars are composed of a mixture of hydrogen, charcoal (carbon), and oxygen.

Lavoisier was also interested in analyzing the mechanism by which sugarcane is transformed into alcohol and carbon dioxide during fermentation. He estimated the proportions of sugars and water at the beginning of the chemical reaction and compared them with the alcohol and carbon dioxide proportions obtained at the end. For the alcoholic reaction to proceed, he also added yeast paste (or "ferment," as it was called). He concluded that sugars were broken down through two chemical pathways: Two-thirds of the sugars were reduced to form alcohol, and the other third were oxidized to form carbon dioxide (the source of the bubbles observed during fermentation). Lavoisier predicted (according to his famous conservation-of-mass principle) that if it was possible to combine alcohol and carbon dioxide in the right proportions, the resulting product would be sugar. The experiment provided a clear insight into the basic chemical reactions needed to produce alcohol. However, there was one problem: Where did the yeast fit into the reaction? The chemists hypothesized that the yeast initiated alcoholic fermentation but did not take part in the reaction. They assumed that the yeast remained unchanged throughout the chemical reactions.

Yeast Are Microorganisms

In 1815 the French chemist Joseph-Louis Gay-Lussac made some interesting observations about yeast. Gay-Lussac was experimenting with a method developed by Nicolas Appert, a confectioner and cooker, for preventing perishable food from rotting. Gay-Lussac was interested in using the method to maintain grape juice wort in an unfermented state for an indefinite time. The method consisted of boiling the wort in a vessel, and then tightly closing the vessel containing the boiling fluid to avoid exposure to air. With this method, the grape juice remained unfermented for long periods as long as the vessel was kept closed. However, if yeast (ferment) was introduced into the wort after the liquid cooled, the wort would begin to ferment. There was now no doubt that yeast were indispensable for alcoholic fermentation. But what role did they play in the process?

When more powerful microscopes were developed, the nature of yeast came to be better understood. In 1835, Charles Cagniard de la Tour, a French inventor, observed that during alcoholic fermentation yeast multiply by gemmation (budding). His observation confirmed that yeast are one-celled organisms and suggested that they were closely related to the fermentation process. Around the same time, Theodor Schwann, Friedrich Kützing, and Christian Erxleben independently concluded that "the globular, or oval, corpuscles which float so thickly in the yeast [ferment] as to make it muddy" were living organisms (Barnett 1998). The recognition that yeast are living entities and not merely organic residues changed the prevailing idea that fermentation was only a chemical process. This discovery paved the way to understand the role of yeast in fermentation.

Pasteur Demonstrates the Role of Yeast in Fermentation

Our modern understanding of the fermentation process comes from the work of the French chemist Louis Pasteur. Pasteur was the first to demonstrate experimentally that fermented beverages result from the action of living yeast transforming glucose into ethanol. Moreover, Pasteur demonstrated that only microorganisms are capable of converting sugars into alcohol from grape juice, and that the process occurs in the absence of oxygen. He concluded that fermentation is a vital process, and he defined it as respiration without air.

Pasteur performed careful experiments and demonstrated that the end products of alcoholic fermentation are more numerous and complex than those initially reported by Lavoisier. Along with alcohol and carbon dioxide, there were also significant amounts of glycerin, succinic acid, and amylic alcohol (some of these molecules were optical isomers — a characteristic of many important molecules required for life). These observations suggested that fermentation was an organic process. To confirm his hypothesis, Pasteur reproduced fermentation under experimental conditions, and his results showed that fermentation and yeast multiplication occur in parallel. He realized that fermentation is a consequence of the yeast multiplication, and the yeast have to be alive for alcohol to be produced. Pasteur published his seminal results in a preliminary paper in 1857 and in a final version in 1860, which was titled "Mémoire sur la fermentation alcoolique".

In 1856, a man named Bigo sought Pasteur's help because he was having problems at his distillery, which produced alcohol from sugar beetroot fermentation. The contents of his fermentation containers were embittered, and instead of alcohol he was obtaining a substance similar to sour milk. Pasteur analyzed the chemical contents of the sour substance and found that it contained a substantial amount of lactic acid instead of alcohol. When he compared the sediments from different containers under the microscope, he noticed that large amounts of yeast were visible in samples from the containers in which alcoholic fermentation had occurred. In contrast, in the polluted containers, the ones containing lactic acid, he observed "much smaller cells than the yeast." Pasteur's finding showed that there are two types of fermentation: alcoholic and lactic acid. Alcoholic fermentation occurs by the action of yeast; lactic acid fermentation, by the action of bacteria.

Isolating the Cell's Chemical Machinery

By the end of the nineteenth century, Eduard Buchner had shown that fermentation could occur in yeast extracts free of cells, making it possible to study fermentation biochemistry in vitro. He prepared cell-free extracts by carefully grinding yeast cells with a pestle and mortar. The resulting moist mixture was put through a press to obtain a "juice" to which sugar was added. Using a microscope, Buchner confirmed that there were no living yeast cells in the extract.

Upon studying the cell-free extracts, Buchner detected zymase, the active constituent of the extracts that carries out fermentation. He realized that the chemical reactions responsible for fermentation were occurring inside the yeast. Today researchers know that zymase is a collection of enzymes (proteins that promote chemical reactions). Enzymes are part of the cellular machinery, and all of the chemical reactions that occur inside cells are catalyzed and modulated by enzymes. For his discoveries, Buchner was awarded the Nobel Prize in Chemistry in 1907.

Around 1929, Karl Lohmann, Yellapragada Subbarao, and Cirus Friske independently discovered an essential molecule called adenosine triphosphate (ATP) in animal tissues. ATP is a versatile molecule used by enzymes and other proteins in many cellular processes. It is required for many chemical reactions, such as sugar degradation and fermentation. In 1941, Fritz Albert Lipmann proposed that ATP was the main energy transfer molecule in the cell.

Sugar Decomposition

Glycolysis — the metabolic pathway that converts glucose (a type of sugar) into pyruvate — is the first major step of fermentation or respiration in cells. It is an ancient metabolic pathway that probably developed about 3.5 billion years ago, when no oxygen was available in the environment. Glycolysis occurs not only in microorganisms, but in every living cell.

Because of its importance, glycolysis was the first metabolic pathway resolved by biochemists. The scientists studying glycolysis faced an enormous challenge as they figured out how many chemical reactions were involved, and the order in which these reactions took place. In glycolysis, a single molecule of glucose (with six carbon atoms) is transformed into two molecules of pyruvic acid (each with three carbon atoms).

In order to understand glycolysis, scientists began by analyzing and purifying the labile component of cell-free extracts, which Buchner called zymase. They also detected a low-molecular-weight, heat-stable molecule, later called cozymase. Using chemical analyses, they learned that zymase is a complex of several enzymes; and cozymase is a mixture of ATP, ADP (adenosine diphosphate, a hydrolyzed form of ATP), metals, and coenzymes (substances that combine with proteins to make them functional), such as NAD+ (nicotinamide adenine dinucleotide). Both components were required for fermentation to occur.

The complete glycolytic pathway, which involves a sequence of ten chemical reactions, was elucidated around 1940. In glycolysis, two molecules of ATP are produced for each broken molecule of glucose. During glycolysis, two reduction-oxidation (redox) reactions occur. In a redox reaction, one molecule is oxidized by losing electrons, while the other molecule is reduced by gaining those electrons. A molecule called NADH acts as the electron carrier in glycolysis, and this molecule must be reconstituted to ensure continuity of the glycolysis pathway.

The Chemical Process of Fermentation

As mentioned above, glucose is converted into pyruvic acid during glycolysis. When oxygen is available, pyruvic acid enters a series of chemical reactions (known as the tricarboxylic acid cycle) and proceeds to the respiratory chain. As a result of respiration, cells produce 36–38 molecules of ATP for each molecule of glucose oxidized.

In the absence of oxygen (anoxygenic conditions), pyruvic acid can follow two different routes, depending on the type of cell. It can be converted into ethanol (alcohol) and carbon dioxide through the alcoholic fermentation pathway, or it can be converted into lactate through the lactic acid fermentation pathway.

Since Pasteur's work, several types of microorganisms (including yeast and some bacteria) have been used to break down pyruvic acid to produce ethanol in beer brewing and wine making. The other by-product of fermentation, carbon dioxide, is used in bread making and the production of carbonated beverages. Other living organisms (such as humans) metabolize pyruvic acid into lactate because they lack the enzymes needed for alcohol production, and in mammals lactate is recycled into glucose by the liver.

Selecting Yeast in Beer Brewing and Wine Making
Humankind has benefited from fermentation products, but from the yeast's point of view, alcohol and carbon dioxide are just waste products. As yeast continues to grow and metabolize sugar, the accumulation of alcohol becomes toxic and eventually kills the cells. Most yeast strains can tolerate an alcohol concentration of 10–15% before being killed. This is why the percentage of alcohol in wines and beers is typically in this concentration range. However, like humans, different strains of yeast can tolerate different amounts of alcohol. Therefore, brewers and wine makers can select different strains of yeast to produce different alcohol contents in their fermented beverages, which range from 5 percent to

21 percent of alcohol by volume. For beverages with higher concentrations of alcohol (like liquors), the fermented products must be distilled.

Summary

Today, beer brewing and wine making are huge, enormously profitable agricultural industries. These industries developed from ancient and empirical knowledge from many different cultures around the world. Today this ancient knowledge has been combined with basic scientific knowledge and applied toward modern production processes. These industries are the result of the laborious work of hundreds of scientists who were curious about how things work.

Ever wonder how yeast ferment barley malt into beer? Or how your muscles keep working when you're exercising so hard that they're very low on oxygen?

Both of these processes can happen thanks to alternative glucose breakdown pathways that occur when normal, oxygen-using (aerobic) cellular respiration is not possible—that is, when oxygen isn't around to act as an acceptor at the end of the electron transport chain. These fermentation pathways consist of glycolysis with some extra reactions tacked on at the end. In yeast, the extra reactions make alcohol, while in your muscles, they make lactic acid.

Fermentation is a widespread pathway, but it is not the only way to get energy from fuels anaerobically (in the absence of oxygen). Some living systems instead use an inorganic molecule other than 0^2, such as sulfate, as a final electron acceptor for an electron transport chain. This process, called anaerobic cellular respiration, is performed by some bacteria and archaea.

Anaerobic cellular respiration
Anaerobic cellular respiration is similar to aerobic cellular respiration in that electrons extracted from a fuel molecule are passed through an electron transport chain, driving A, T, P, synthesis. Some organisms use sulfate as the final electron acceptor at the end ot the transport

chain, while others use nitrate, sulfur, or one of a variety of other molecules[1].

What kinds of organisms use anaerobic cellular respiration? Some prokaryotes—bacteria and archaea—that live in low-oxygen environments rely on anaerobic respiration to break down fuels. For example, some archaea called methanogens can use carbon dioxide as a terminal electron acceptor, producing methane as a by-product. Methanogens are found in soil and in the digestive systems of ruminants, a group of animals including cows and sheep.

Similarly, sulfate-reducing bacteria and Archaea use sulfate as a terminal electron acceptor, producing hydrogen sulfide (H_2S) as a byproduct. The image below is an aerial photograph of coastal waters, and the green patches indicate an overgrowth of sulfate-reducing bacteria.

Fermentation

Fermentation is another anaerobic (non-oxygen-requiring) pathway for breaking down glucose, one that's performed by many types of organisms and cells. In fermentation, the only energy extraction pathway is glycolysis, with one or two extra reactions tacked on at the end.

Fermentation and cellular respiration begin the same way, with glycolysis. In fermentation, however, the pyruvate made in glycolysis does not continue through oxidation and the citric acid cycle, and the electron transport chain does not run. Because the electron transport chain isn't functional, the NADH made in glycolysis cannot drop its electrons off there to turn back into NAD+

The purpose of the extra reactions in fermentation, then, is to regenerate the electron carrier NAD+ from the NADH produced in glycolysis. The extra reactions accomplish this by letting NADH drop its electrons off with an organic molecule (such as pyruvate, the end product of glycolysis). This drop-off allows glycolysis to keep running by ensuring a steady supply of NAD+

Lactic acid fermentation

In lactic acid fermentation, NADH transfers its electrons directly to pyruvate, generating lactate as a byproduct. Lactate, which is just the deprotonated form of lactic acid, gives the process its name. The bacteria that make yogurt carry out lactic acid fermentation, as do the red blood cells in your body, which don't have mitochondria and thus can't perform cellular respiration.

Muscle cells also carry out lactic acid fermentation, though only when they have too little oxygen for aerobic respiration to continue—for instance, when you've been exercising very hard. It was once thought that the accumulation of lactate in muscles was responsible for soreness caused by exercise, but recent research suggests this is probably not the case.

Lactic acid produced in muscle cells is transported through the bloodstream to the liver, where it's converted back to pyruvate and processed normally in the remaining reactions of cellular respiration.

Alcohol fermentation

Another familiar fermentation process is alcohol fermentation, in which NADH donates its electrons to a derivative of pyruvate, producing ethanol.

Going from pyruvate to ethanol is a two-step process. In the first step, a carboxyl group is removed from pyruvate and released in as carbon dioxide, producing a two-carbon molecule called acetaldehyde. In the second step, NADH passes its electrons to acetaldehyde, regenerating NAD+ and forming ethanol.

Alcohol fermentation by yeast produces the ethanol found in alcoholic drinks like beer and wine. However, alcohol is toxic to yeasts in large quantities (just as it is to humans), which puts an upper limit on the percentage alcohol in these drinks. Ethanol tolerance of yeast ranges from about 5 percent to 21 percent, depending on the yeast strain and environmental conditions.

Facultative and obligate anaerobes

Many bacteria and archaea are facultative anaerobes, meaning they can switch between aerobic respiration and anaerobic pathways (fermentation or anaerobic respiration) depending on the availability of oxygen. This approach allows lets them get more ATP out of their glucose molecules when oxygen is around—since aerobic cellular respiration makes more ATP than anaerobic pathways—but to keep metabolizing and stay alive when oxygen is scarce.

Other bacteria and archaea are obligate anaerobes, meaning they can live and grow only in the absence of oxygen. Oxygen is toxic to these microorganisms and injures or kills them on exposure. For instance, the Clostridium bacteria that are responsible for botulism (a form of food poisoning) are obligate anaerobes.

Recently, some multicellular animals have even been discovered in deep-sea sediments that are free of oxygen.

Different Types of Fermentation and 6 Tips For Homemade Fermentation

Humanity has been fermenting food since the Neolithic age, long before people understood the science behind the process. Today, following the scientific discoveries of French microbiologist Louis Pasteur, who showed that living organisms initiate fermentation, we know why fermentation not only makes food like sourdough bread, cheese, and wine taste better, but also helps to keep us alive.

How Does Fermentation Work?

To master fermentation, you need to understand the science behind the chemical process.

- Microorganisms survive using carbohydrates (sugars, such as glucose) for energy and fuel.

- Organic chemicals like adenosine triphosphate (ATP) deliver that energy to every part of a cell when needed.

- Microbes generate ATP using respiration. Aerobic respiration, which requires oxygen, is the most efficient way to do that. Aerobic respiration begins with glycolysis, where glucose is converted into pyruvic acid. When there's enough oxygen present, aerobic respiration occurs.

- Fermentation is similar to anaerobic respiration— the kind that takes place when there isn't enough oxygen present. However, fermentation leads to the production of different organic molecules like lactic acid, which also leads to ATP, unlike respiration, which uses pyruvic acid.

- Depending upon environmental conditions, individual cells and microbes have the ability to switch between the two different modes of energy production.

- Organisms commonly obtain energy anaerobically through fermentation, but some systems use sulfate as the final electron acceptor in the electron transport chain.

What Happens During the Fermentation Process?

Fermentation occurs in the absence of oxygen (anaerobic conditions), and in the presence of benecial microorganisms (yeasts, molds, and bacteria) that obtain their energy through fermentation. If enough sugar is available, some yeast cells, such as Saccharomyces cerevisiae, prefer fermentation to aerobic respiration even when oxygen is abundant.

During the fermentation process, these benecial microbes break down sugars and starches into alcohols and acids, making food more nutritious and preserving it so people can store it for longer periods of time without it spoiling.

Fermentation products provide enzymes necessary for digestion. This is important because humans are born with a nite number of enzymes, and they decrease with age. Fermented foods contain the enzymes required to break them down.

Fermentation also aids in pre-digestion. During the fermentation process, the microbes feed on sugars and starches, breaking down food before anyone's even consumed it.

What Are the Advantages of Fermentation?
Fermented foods are rich in probiotics, beneficial microorganisms that help maintain a healthy gut so it can extract nutrients from food.

Probiotics aid the immune system because the gut produces antibiotic, anti-tumor, anti-viral, and antifungal substances, and pathogens don't do well in the acidic environment fermented foods create.

Fermentation also helps neutralize anti-nutrients like phytic acid, which occurs in grains, nuts, seeds, and legumes and can cause mineral deficiencies. Phytates also make starches, proteins, and fats less digestible, so neutralizing them is extremely beneficial.

Fermentation can increase the vitamins and minerals in food and make them more available for absorption. Fermentation increases B and C vitamins and enhances folic acid, riboflavin, niacin, thiamin, and biotin. The probiotics, enzymes, and lactic acid in fermented foods facilitate the absorption of these vitamins and minerals into the body.

What Are the 3 Different Types of Fermentation?

Microbes specialized at converting certain substances into others can produce a variety of foodstuffs and beverages. These are three distinct types of fermentation that people use.

Lactic acid fermentation. Yeast strains and bacteria convert starches or sugars into lactic acid, requiring no heat in preparation. These anaerobic chemical reactions, pyruvic acid uses nicotinamide adenine dinucleotide + hydrogen (NADH) to form lactic acid and NAD+. (Lactic acid fermentation also occurs in human muscle cells. During strenuous activity, muscles can expend adenosine triphosphate (ATP) faster than oxygen can be supplied to muscle cells, resulting in lactic acid buildup and sore muscles. In this scenario, glycolysis, which breaks down a glucose molecule into two pyruvate molecules and doesn't use oxygen, produces ATP.) Lactic acid bacteria are vital to producing and preserving inexpensive, wholesome foods, which is especially important in feeding impoverished populations. This method makes sauerkraut, pickles, kimchi, yogurt, and sourdough bread.

Ethanol fermentation/alcohol fermentation. Yeasts break pyruvate molecules—the output of the metabolism of glucose (C6H12O6) known as glycolysis—in starches or sugars down into alcohol and carbon dioxide molecules. Alcoholic fermentation produces wine and beer.

Acetic acid fermentation. Starches and sugars from grains and fruit ferment into sour tasting vinegar and condiments. Examples include apple cider vinegar, wine vinegar, and kombucha.

What Are the Different Stages of the Fermentation Process?

Depending upon what you're fermenting, the process can have several stages.

Primary fermentation. In this brief phase, microbes begin rapidly working on raw ingredients such as fruit, vegetables, or dairy. The microbes present or in the surrounding liquid (such as brine for fermented vegetables) prevent putrefying bacteria from colonizing the food instead. Yeasts or other microbes convert carbohydrates (sugars) into other substances such as alcohols and acids.

Secondary fermentation. In this longer stage of fermentation, which lasts several days or even weeks, alcohol levels rise and yeasts and microbes die off and their available food source (the carbohydrates) becomes scarcer. Winemakers and brewers use secondary fermentation to create their alcoholic beverages. The pH of the ferment can differ significantly from when it started out, which affects the chemical reactions taking place between the microbes and their environment. Once alcohol is between 12–15% and it kills the yeast, preventing further fermentation, distillation is needed to remove water, condensing alcohol content to create a higher percentage of alcohol (proof).

Tips for Starting Fermentation
Whether you're looking to pickle vegetables or begin brewing beer at home, these tips will help you start fermenting. S

1. Establish your "starter" cultures. Microbes are naturally present in the air you breathe, but to begin fermentation you will often need a "starter" set of cultures, such as whey (from yogurt), a Symbiotic Colony of Bacteria and Yeast, or SCOBY (for kombucha), or even liquid from a previous ferment. Starter cultures are already rich with benecial microorganisms. When you add them to your food or beverage product, they'll multiply rapidly and jump-start the fermentation process.

2. Keep your equipment clean. To prevent bad bacteria from leaching onto your ferment, it's essential that you clean and sterilize your kitchen equipment and the surfaces that you work on.

3. Avoid exposure. Exposing your ferment to air can prevent proper fermentation from taking place and increase the risk of spoilage and food poisoning. There are several ways you can avoid that.

4. To prevent fermenting food from coming into contact with air, you can submerge it in a salt solution (brine). When fermenting solid pieces of food like chopped vegetables, this method works well. You can control the pH of the fermentation, which determines how much oxygen will be present, by adding vinegar to your solution.

5. Storage. To avoid air contamination, you should keep your fermenting product in a sealable storage container. Many home fermenters use a simple mason jar with a lid to lock out air, but there are other alternatives. Typically, storage containers have a valve to vent carbon dioxide gas

released during fermentation. If you are committed to carefully monitoring your ferment so it doesn't spoil, you can alternatively open sealed containers manually to release the carbon dioxide. (If you are making kombucha, wine, or other end products that benefit from carbonation, you can forgo the CO2 venting.)

6. Fermentation management. By controlling the temperature of the environment, you can affect the outcome of your fermentation. Typically, microbes work well when their environment is warm or room temperature, but the ideal temperature depends upon the type of microbes you're using and what you're fermenting. Altering the temperature can impact your process greatly. Moving your product to a cooler environment, such as a basement or a refrigerator, will slow the rate of fermentation and, in some cases, halt it completely. Heating a ferment, on the other hand, can kill your essential microbes.

www.ingramcontent.com/pod-product-compliance
Lightning Source LLC
Chambersburg PA
CBHW070323160726
47999CB00003B/1125